God's World

Daily Devotions at Advent

Arthur Boers

Church Health Center
Memphis, TN

About the Church Health Center
The Church Health Center seeks to reclaim the church's biblical commitment to care for our bodies and our spirits. Long recognized as a national model for serving the uninsured, the Center has spent years connecting people of faith and their congregations with quality health resources and educational experiences. To learn more about the Center, visit ChurchHealthCenter.org. To learn more about our magazine on health ministry, *Church Health Reader*, visit chreader.org.

About the Author
Rev. Dr. Arthur Boers holds the R. J. Bernardo Family Chair of Leadership at Tyndale Seminary (Toronto, Canada). He previously taught pastoral theology at Associated Mennonite Biblical Seminary (Elkhart, Indiana). An ordained minister and Benedictine oblate, he served for over sixteen years as a pastor in rural, urban, and church-planting settings in the USA and Canada. His newest book is *Living into Focus: Choosing What Matters in an Age of Distractions* (Brazos, 2012), and he is the author of *The Way is Made by Walking: A Pilgrimage Along the Camino de Santiago* (InterVarsity, 2007) reflecting on a 500-mile pilgrimage that he walked in Spain. His work has appeared in *Christian Century*, *Christianity Today*, *America*, and *Church Health Reader*.

Our Work, God's World: Daily Devotions at Advent © 2012 Church Health Center, Inc. Memphis, TN

Second Printing, 2013

Scripture quotations contained herein are from the New Revised Standard Version Bible, copyright 1989, Division of Christian Education of the National Council of the Churches of Christ in the United States of America, and are used by permission. All rights reserved.

ISBN: 978-1-62144-029-1

Printed in the United States of America

Design and layout by Lizy Heard

The primary objective of *Our Work, God's World: Daily Devotions at Advent* is to help you and your community to consider how work and faith intersect in their lives during the season of Advent. We have bulk discounts available to encourage group use in your congregation.

The Church Health Center welcomes your feedback. Please send your comments to FCO@churchhealthcenter.org.

Introduction

One impressive aspect about Advent is the fact that so many Scriptural characters are not that impressive. They would not be noticed by the important people of their day. They are normal folks, going about daily chores, activities, duties, business, and work. Yet God dramatically intervenes in their lives, such that world history itself is affected.

You and I still benefit from the choices made by regular folks—Zechariah, Elizabeth, Mary, Joseph, and John the Baptizer. While Zechariah met God's messenger as he went about religious duties, as far as we can tell Mary, Joseph, and Elizabeth encountered God's messengers in their routine. John the Baptizer, of course, led a dramatic and exceptional life, but did not call others to be like him; he asked people to live faithfully where they were already located.

Christians believe that life is not divided into sacred (religious duties) and ordinary (daily life). As L. Colin Owens says: "today is the only place we can encounter Christ" (*Abba, Give Me a Word*, Paraclete 2012, page 129).

God can meet us always and everywhere. Advent is about waiting for God to take on human flesh ("incarnation") and joining our routine realities—inside and beyond the home. May these devotionals help us to seek God and God's priorities through the responsibilities that are ours—whether jobs or volunteer commitments or school or neighborhood involvements.

Advent 1
Zechariah: A Dutiful Man

*Immediately his mouth was opened and his tongue
freed, and he began to speak, praising God.*
—Luke 1:64

This week, we reflect on the work, life, and witness of Zechariah—an old man and little known priest—and also begin to encounter his spouse, Elizabeth, a housewife. Just plain folks, they nevertheless are the parents of John the Baptizer. Zechariah is also given credit for one of the most well known songs of praise in the New Testament, the *Benedictus* (Luke 1:66–79). Many Christians pray with Zechariah's song every single morning.

Sunday

In the days of King Herod of Judea, there was a priest named Zechariah, who belonged to the priestly order of Abijah. His wife was a descendant of Aaron, and her name was Elizabeth. Both of them were righteous before God, living blamelessly according to all the commandments and regulations of the Lord. But they had no children, because Elizabeth was barren, and both were getting on in years.
—Luke 1:5–7

Reflection

This story moves from a brief mention of the high and famous (King Herod of Judea) to a detailed description of a little known clergy person and his wife. In their culture's eyes, the main thing they have going for them is ancestry. And the main thing they have going against them is that they have no children. Many would therefore suspect that they did not find favor with God.

Zechariah is doing work handed down to him by his forebears; Elizabeth too is steeped in her family's traditions. In God's eyes, they were commendable because of the fact that they lived "blamelessly," following God's commandments and regulations. This narrative invites us to see others and ourselves from God's perspectives, God's eyes.

To Ponder

How do your neighbors and our culture perceive your roles?

In what ways are you and those close to you significant to God?

Prayer

Advent Savior,
who comes to be with us,
we hear the voices of what others think of us—
our roles, our appearance,
our responsibilities, our age, our race.
Let this Advent be a season
when we can look at all we are and do
in light of how you regard us.
Amen.

Monday

*Once when [Zechariah] was serving as priest before
God and his section was on duty, he was chosen by
lot, according to the custom of the priesthood, to
enter the sanctuary of the Lord and offer incense.*
—Luke 1:8–9

Reflection

Zechariah honors his responsibilities. We have already seen that
he and Elizabeth live "blamelessly," faithfully following God's laws.
In today's Scripture excerpt, he is working with fellow priests. His
job is important, "to enter the sanctuary and offer incense." But
he does not get to do this because of any achievements of his own.
Rather, he is a priest because of his family and offers incense because
he is "chosen by lot." No extraordinary accomplishments here.

Duty, *obligation* and *responsibility* are words that do not get a
lot of respect in our day. Yet Christians throughout the ages have
taught that we often encounter God by honoring commitments,
both those we take on and those passed on to us.

To Ponder

What roles and responsibilities have you chosen or inherited?

Where and how have you met God in living up to obligations?

Prayer

Advent Savior,
who comes to be with us,
you have not created us by accident,
nor have you just happened to locate us
in our particular families and situations,
neighborhoods and communities.
Today as we live out commitments and responsibilities,
help us to see how you have entrusted them to us.
Amen.

Tuesday

Then there appeared to him an angel of the Lord,
standing at the right side of the altar of incense.
When Zechariah saw him, he was terrified, and fear
overwhelmed him. But the angel said to him: "Do
not be afraid, Zechariah, for your prayer has been
heard. Your wife Elizabeth will bear you a son, and
you will name him John. You will have joy and
gladness and many will rejoice at his birth, for he
will be great in the sight of the Lord."
—Luke 1:11–15

Reflection

Zechariah does not expect to have such a vividly religious experience while fulfilling *religious* duties and obligations! So he reacts to the angel's appearance with terror and fright. Actually, in the Bible this is the usual response to angels. Nevertheless, the angel brings good news: Zechariah's fervent prayer being heard and answered, "joy and gladness" not only for Zechariah and his wife but a child who will cause many to rejoice.

If it is true that "today is the only place we can encounter Christ" (*Abba, Give Me a Word*, page 129), then we need to pay closer attention in our daily life. At the job, in school, while volunteering, working at home—are all locations where a messenger of God (the literal meaning of *angel*) might show up with an important word.

To Ponder

Is there a responsibility today that you dread or fear?

Name one concern you fervently want God to address.

Prayer

Advent Savior,
who comes to be with us,
help us this day to be alert
and to pay attention to you and your messengers.
In the places where we are afraid,
help us to find the joy and gladness
you long to give.
Amen.

Wednesday

Zechariah said to the angel, "How will I know that this is so? For I am an old man, and my wife is getting on in years." The angel replied, "I am Gabriel. I stand in the presence of God, and I have been sent to speak to you and to bring you this good news. But now, because you did not believe my words, which will be fulfilled in their time, you will become mute, unable to speak, until the day these things occur." Meanwhile the people were waiting for Zechariah and wondered at his delay in the sanctuary. When he did come out, he could not speak to them, and they realized that he had seen a vision in the sanctuary. He kept motioning to them and remained unable to speak. When his time of service was ended, he went to his home.
—Luke 1:18–23

Reflection

I always feel badly for Zechariah. Out of the blue he learns that even though he is aged and his wife is "getting on in years," they are about to have a child. (We are supposed to remember Abraham and Sarah here.) He has trouble taking this in or believing it. He wants proof or evidence, some kind of guarantee, a sign. For that he is punished by being made mute. The sign he gets is his own silence. And then, after all this trauma, he gets to keep working until "his time of service was ended." But, as we have seen, he dutifully fulfilled responsibilities.

Zechariah's story reminds us that divine encounters are not always fun and games. This vision starts with fear and ends with being made mute. Jacob wrestled for a blessing and came away with a permanent hip wound. Meeting God in daily life, in the midst of our duties, might call us to places we would rather not go, to things we would rather not do, to realities we would rather not face. As the old saying goes, "Be careful what you pray for."

To Ponder

Which promises of God have you found hard to believe?

How has God changed or challenged you in surprising ways?

Prayer

Advent Savior,
who comes to be with us,
on our own we are not able
to fully face our responsibilities,
to do what we are called to do.
Help us this day not just to trust
and believe in your promises,
but to root ourselves and our actions
in everything that you make possible.
Amen.

Thursday

They began motioning to his father [Zechariah] to find out what name he wanted to give to him. He asked for a writing tablet and wrote, "His name is John." And all of them were amazed. Immediately his mouth was opened and his tongue freed, and he began to speak, praising God. Fear came over all their neighbors, and all these things were talked about throughout the entire hill country of Judea.
—Luke 1:62–65

Reflection

Elizabeth and Zechariah do not hesitate to obey the angel by naming their son John. Yet they are going against tradition; none of their family has this name. With this faithful act, Zechariah's speech is recovered and what a speech he makes, praising God's wonders and goodness. He has had a long time to ponder his thoughts. Meanwhile, neighbors and relatives who at first rejoiced (verse 58) quickly move to fear and gossip.

Zechariah and Elizabeth are made strong and resolute by involvement with God. They do not have to follow family and cultural traditions about naming their son. They can live in ways that cause fear and uneasiness among those nearby.

To Ponder

Discuss a time when you felt deep gratitude to God.

Where in your daily life does faithfulness risk making you misunderstood?

Prayer

Advent Savior,
who comes to be with us,
teach us to live in ways that help us honor you.
Teach us to have words of praise for you.
Teach us to overcome fear of what others think,
so that we know how to live in obedience to you.
Amen.

Friday

*Then his father Zechariah was filled with the
Holy Spirit and spoke this prophecy:
"Blessed be the Lord God of Israel,
for he has looked favorably on his people and
redeemed them.
He has raised up a mighty savior for us
in the house of his servant David,
as he spoke through the mouth of his holy prophets
from of old … ."*
—Luke 1:67–70

Reflection

This is an excerpt of the prophecy that Zechariah spoke. It resembles a psalm and is often described as Zechariah's Canticle. (Liturgical Christians call it by a Latin name, "Benedictus.") Astonishingly, many Christians recite, sing, or pray this entire passage every day, often in their morning prayers.

Zechariah performs small acts of faithfulness—doing his duty at work, naming the child as the angel predicted, following religious obligations in bringing up the child. Yet God works through him and his wife in ways that richly benefited everyone. Sometimes we hope God will bless us for our own advantages and advances. While Elizabeth and Zechariah are richly blessed, it is so that they could and would share God's blessings with others.

To Ponder

Name ways that God blessed you through the faithfulness of others.

Where is one place where you can represent God's blessing today?

Prayer

Advent Savior,
who comes to be with us,
teach us to be people of praise,
like your faithful servant Zechariah.
May our hearts, our lips, our lives, and our work
bring you glory.
Amen.

Saturday

"By the tender mercy of our God,
the dawn from on high will break upon us,
to give light to those who sit in darkness
and in the shadow of death,
to guide our feet into the way of peace."
—Luke 1:78–79

Reflection

These concluding lines of Zechariah's Canticle of praise summarize the themes, promises, and prophecies of Advent: God's mercy, light to those in the dark and facing death, guiding us into the ways of God's peace. Consider memorizing these lines (or the whole Canticle) and using it as a prayer every day.

Advent means "coming." In this season, we remember how God came to us in the person of Jesus. We also anticipate how Jesus will come again and bring God's reign in its fullness. And we are given opportunity for God to work in our lives, whatever our roles and responsibilities.

To Ponder

Name broken places in our world that need God's healing, help, and intervention.

What can you do today to demonstrate God's hope to others?

Prayer

Advent Savior,
who comes to be with us,
we live in a hurting and broken world.
We need your help!
May we learn not just to trust in your promises
but to live in ways this day that show your mercy,
bring your light, and reflect your peace.
Amen.

Advent 2

Elizabeth and Joseph:
Partners to Their Spouses and with God

*"And why has this happened to me, that the mother
of my Lord comes to me?"*
—Luke 1:43

In this second week of Advent, we ponder the example of Elizabeth, Zechariah's partner, and Joseph, Mary's partner. While Elizabeth is not as well known as her son—and does not have a dramatic encounter with an angel, as Zechariah did—she is able to see how God works in her life. And while Joseph is often overshadowed by Mary in Christmas stories, God uses him and his loyal faithfulness to accomplish God's purposes.

Sunday

After those days his wife Elizabeth conceived, and for five months she remained in seclusion. She said, "This is what the Lord has done for me when he looked favorably on me and took away the disgrace I have endured among my people."
—Luke 1:24–25

Reflection

Like Zechariah, Elizabeth is aging. Unlike him, her life is lived out more privately. Honoring home responsibilities, she shows a lively and vital faith and finds herself inspired by the Holy Spirit. This short passage indicates several aspects of how that culture then differs from our settings. For one thing, Elizabeth is in seclusion, hiding her pregnancy. When my mother was a child (she was the eldest) she was not even aware when her mother was pregnant. Now we are more open about pregnancies. Elizabeth's previous inability to have a child is for her a matter of disgrace. While we no longer consider lack of children a stigma, many people feel great sadness when they are unable to be fertile in this way.

Elizabeth is a believer in her own right. She does not just follow religious rules and rituals because her husband is a minister. Rather she interprets her life in terms of God's goodness and purposes. She is able to see God working in her circumstances.

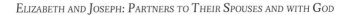
To Ponder

Name places where you have seen God working this past week.

Where in your life would you like to see God's intervention?

Prayer

Advent Savior,
who comes to be with us,
we marvel at the faithfulness of your servant Elizabeth.
Help us to pay attention to where you are at work in our
lives,
so that we might give you the credit that you deserve
and we might live in ways that bring you glory.
Amen.

Monday

When Elizabeth heard Mary's greeting, the child
leaped in her womb. And Elizabeth was filled with
the Holy Spirit and exclaimed with a loud cry,
"Blessed are you among women, and blessed is the
fruit of your womb. … And blessed is she who
believed that there would be a fulfillment of what
was spoken to her by the Lord."
—Luke 1:41–42, 45

Reflection

Young Mary and aging Elizabeth are relatives (Luke 1:36) with many things in common. They are both miraculously and mysteriously pregnant—one a virgin, the other an old woman. They both have a lively relationship with God. No wonder they want to be together, compare notes, offer each other support.

Even though she herself is richly blessed by God, Elizabeth commends Mary. Elizabeth is the more senior, and her pregnancy is more advanced, yet she directs her goodwill toward what God is doing through Mary and toward Mary's faithfulness. It is an astonishingly selfless move.

To Ponder

Name someone in your family, neighborhood, church or community who inspires you by his or her faithfulness.

How can you encourage another believer today?

Prayer

Advent Savior,
who comes to be with us,
you are active in the lives of many around us.
Help us to see where you are at work
and teach us how to bless, affirm and encourage
those who trust in you.
Amen.

Tuesday

"And why has this happened to me, that the mother of my Lord comes to me? For as soon as I heard the sound of your greeting, the child in my womb leaped for joy."
—Luke 1:43–44

Reflection

While Elizabeth appropriately focuses on the faithfulness of Mary, she nevertheless also sees that God is at work in her own life too. In verse 25 (which we looked at on Sunday) and here again, she testifies about God's intervention on her behalf.

A classic Christian prayer exercise involves reviewing one's day in the evening and considering all the places where one has been touched by God or drawn to God. Usually when I undertake this discipline, I am surprised by the many ways that God blesses me. Elizabeth embodies gratitude for God's good work.

To Ponder

Name and describe someone who exemplifies gratitude and joy.

Where have you been blessed or drawn by God in the last 24 hours?

Prayer

Advent Savior,
who comes to be with us,
why has this happened to us,
that you bless us in so many ways?
Teach us how to speak gratefully
of all you have done on our behalf.
Amen.

Wednesday

*On the eighth day they came to circumcise the child, and
they were going to name him Zechariah after his father.
But his mother said, "No; he is to be called John."*
—Luke 1:59–60

Reflection

This passage leaves more questions than answers. Had Zechariah
told Elizabeth (by writing since he couldn't speak) that the baby
was to be named John? What had he written for her about his
angel encounter? In a culture where women were often regarded
as inferior, what gave her the strength and courage to stand against
tradition and award her son an unprecedented name?

As far as we can tell, Elizabeth is a homebody. Zechariah
encounters an angel in the sanctuary but Elizabeth stays home,
waiting for her husband's return. Pregnant, she goes into seclusion.
When Mary wanted to see Elizabeth, she has to travel to Elizabeth's
house. When it is time for circumcision, others came to Elizabeth.
Yet Elizabeth is so securely rooted in her experience of God that
she could not be budged from what she knew to be best: the baby
should be called John even though no one in the family tree had
that name.

To Ponder

Describe a place in your life where you feel pressure to act in a way that is counter to God's will.

Where do you need courage to be more resolute?

Prayer

Advent Savior,
who comes to be with us,
Elizabeth stands firm in the face of pressure.
Help us to know what you want us to do
and how you want us to live,
and help us do so with firmness and grace.
Amen.

Thursday

*[Mary's] husband Joseph, being a righteous man and
unwilling to expose her to public disgrace, planned
to dismiss her quietly.*
—Matthew 1:19

Reflection

We do not know much about Joseph. He is often thought to be
older than Mary. We read a little about him in Advent and
Christmas accounts. After that, he appears only once more in a
story that takes place when Jesus is 12. And then we never hear
more from or about the man.

He is honorable, "righteous" the text says. Like Zechariah and
Elizabeth, he knows about duty, and he honors responsibilities.
Understandably, he is reluctant to stay engaged to Mary when she
becomes pregnant. But even here he behaves with restraint,
planning "to dismiss her quietly." He does not act self-righteously
or arrogantly; he is not bent on revenge. He tries to do the right
thing as he best understands it.

To Ponder

When have you felt justifiably righteous?

Where has someone shown you unexpected mercy?

Prayer

Advent Savior,
who comes to be with us,
we understand Joseph's reluctance to keep Mary as his fiancée.
But we are challenged by his commitment to be righteous,
even when he had reason to feel hurt and betrayed.
Teach us to act and live with that kind of gentleness, we ask.
Amen.

Friday

*But just when [Joseph] had resolved to do this, an angel
of the Lord appeared to him in a dream and said,
"Joseph, son of David, do not be afraid to take Mary as
your wife, for the child conceived in her is from the
Holy Spirit. She will bear a son, and you are to name
him Jesus, for he will save his people from their sins."
. . . . When Joseph awoke from sleep, he did as the angel
of the Lord commanded him; he took her as his wife,
but had no marital relations with her until she had
borne a son; and he named him Jesus.*
—Matthew 1:20–21, 24–25

Reflection

Like Joseph of the Old Testament, this Joseph also hears God
through dreams. Mary's husband would obey other dreams too
(Matthew 2:13; 2:19). And like Zechariah, Elizabeth, Mary, and
John the Baptizer, he has lively interaction with God. But it is a
unique relationship. Joseph does not run into angels in a sanctuary
or feel the Holy Spirit in his body; he dreams of an angel.

Like Elizabeth and Zechariah, Joseph exemplifies obedience
and responsibility. Once he understands God's will, he does not
hesitate to do as instructed. Not only does he wed Mary, he also
gives her son the name that the angel commanded.

To Ponder

Is there a difficult challenge facing you today?

What do you need from God that would help you be more faithful?

Prayer

Advent Savior,
who comes to be with us,
Joseph is able to undertake the difficult challenge
you put before him.
Help us to learn from his example,
to have that kind of courage,
to trust in you.
Amen.

Saturday

*All this took place to fulfill what had been spoken by
the Lord through the prophet:
"Look, the virgin shall conceive and bear a son,
and they shall name him Emmanuel,"
which means, "God is with us."*
—Matthew 1:22–23

Reflection

In Joseph's profoundly theological dream, he learns that Mary's pregnancy fulfilled ancient prophecy. This is a key verse of the Advent-Christmas story.

The promise in this dream is that God will be with us, be in solidarity with us, be present with us. In Jesus, God takes on human flesh and became like us. We are no longer alone in our pain and sorrow and suffering. This grand promise apparently made all the difference for Joseph too.

To Ponder

Has God ever spoken to you through a dream?

Where would you right now like a clearer sense of God's will or purpose?

Prayer

Advent Savior,
who comes to be with us,
we thank you for the great gift
of your becoming one of us.
Help us to remember we are not alone
and to take comfort in the fact
that you are with us.
Amen.

Advent 3
Mary: The Servant of the Lord

"Here am I, the servant of the Lord; let it be with
me according to your word."
—Luke 1:38

Besides Jesus, Mary is the most visible person in the Advent and Christmas texts. At first we know her better than Jesus, as we see her in action and hear her words. This week we consider how her example inspires our faithfulness.

Sunday

In the sixth month the angel Gabriel was sent by God to a town in Galilee called Nazareth to a virgin engaged to a man whose name was Joseph, of the house of David. The virgin's name was Mary. And he came to her and said, "Greetings, favored one! The Lord is with you." But she was much perplexed by his words and pondered what sort of greeting this might be. The angel said to her, "Do not be afraid, Mary, for you have found favor with God."
—Luke 1:26–30

Reflection

We do not know much about Mary's circumstances. Is she doing routine housework when this happened? Is she praying? We elsewhere heard about the good character of Zechariah, Elizabeth, and Joseph, but not much is told about Mary—except that for some reason she "found favor with God." We do not know how old she is, although tradition often suggests that she was probably a teenager. Not surprisingly, she is perplexed by this encounter. Just as Zechariah was unsettled by the angel's appearance, Mary is flummoxed by what happens to her. Gabriel has to tell her—as he previously told Zechariah—not to fear.

Yesterday we recalled the angel's promise to Joseph about Emmanuel, or "God is with us." Today we see that the angel promises Mary, "The Lord is with you." As all the characters in these stories can attest, God's presence turns our worlds upside down and our lives inside out.

To Ponder

Describe a time when you felt God's favor or blessing.

Where do you fear that God might want to make a radical change or shake-up in your life?

Prayer

Advent Savior,
who comes to be with us,
we are moved by the beauty of Gabriel's encounter with
Mary, an encounter that catches her off guard.
Help us to be open to the many ways
that you will speak to us today and this week.
Amen.

Monday

*"And now, you will conceive in your womb and bear
a son, and you will name him Jesus. He will be
great, and will be called the Son of the Most High,
and the Lord God will give to him the throne of his
ancestor David. He will reign over the house of Jacob
forever, and of his kingdom there will be no end."*
—Luke 1:31–33

Reflection

What do you suppose Mary makes of these exalted promises? No
wonder she is perplexed. We might be matter-of-fact about these
words as we have heard them so often. But neither Mary nor
anyone she knows had ever heard anything quite like this. A
teenager in an out-of-the-way town giving birth to a king who
would reign forever!

These few verses are loaded with God's promises of what God
is going to do: the baby will be named Jesus (meaning "salvation"
or "rescue"), he will be "great" and "Son of the Most High" and
his reign will be endless. Mary could not take that all in and, truth
be told, neither can we. That's one reason why we keep observing
Advent and celebrating Christmas year after year.

To Ponder

Which promise about Jesus in today's text most inspires you? Why?

Where do you see the need for God's help today?

Prayer

Advent Savior,
who comes to be with us,
as we continue to ponder
the many and marvelous promises of Advent,
help us to see them as promises
for us, our lives, and our world too.
Please bring your rescuing help
to the needs we named today.
Amen.

Tuesday

Mary said to the angel, "How can this be, since I am a virgin?" The angel said to her, "The Holy Spirit will come upon you, and the power of the Most High will overshadow you; therefore the child to be born will be holy; he will be called the Son of God. And now, your relative Elizabeth in her old age has also conceived a son; and this is the sixth month for her who was said to be barren. For nothing will be impossible with God."
—Luke 1:34–38

Reflection

When Zechariah inquired about the miracle of his wife's pregnancy, he was struck mute. We are not sure why. Was it his request for a sign? Was a pregnant wife enough of a sign?

Mary also wonders how a miraculous pregnancy could be and is reassured of another wondrous conception and told that nothing is impossible with God. She is not punished but is given a sign, without even asking for one!

To Ponder

Where do you find it hard to trust whether God is at work?

What question would you like to pose to God or an angel of God's?

Prayer

Advent Savior,
who comes to be with us,
we hardly know what to make of the extraordinary things
that happen to Mary.
Teach us to discern what you are doing
here in our world and among us today.
Amen.

Wednesday

*Then Mary said, "Here am I, the servant of the
Lord; let it be with me according to your word."
Then the angel departed from her.*
—Luke 1:38

Reflection

This can rightly be regarded as one of Advent's most important
verses. Mary fully acquiesces to God's will. She is willing to serve
God and obey what she hears. Luke later has an inside joke in
connection with this text. In chapter 8, we read that the mother
and brothers of Jesus came to see him and he responds, "My mother
and my brothers are those who hear the word of God and do it."
Today's text shows that Mary is literally the first disciple of Jesus—
she hears the word of God and obeys. No wonder so many
Christians admired her through the ages.

I love the detail that the angel does not stay. As soon as Mary
accepts and agrees, she is left alone. Obedience to God does not
guarantee that we will be consoled by divine company.

To Ponder

Where are you wrestling with how hard it is to obey God?

What would it take for you to risk more on behalf of God's priorities?

Prayer

Advent Savior,
who comes to be with us,
teach us, inspire us, and mold us
so that we can be more like Mary's faithful trusting of you.
We ask not only that you show us your will
but that you help us to obey you as well.
Amen.

Thursday

In those days Mary set out and went with haste to a
Judean town in the hill country, where she entered
the house of Zechariah and greeted Elizabeth.
—Luke 1:39

Reflection

When my wife was pregnant, one of her great joys was that two of
her closest friends were with child at the same time. She savored
comparing notes with them as they talked about symptoms and
challenges, hopes and fears, physical changes and emotional turmoil.
Not surprising then that Mary would visit a pregnant relative.

Their connection went even deeper. Not only were both
pregnancies miraculous, both women had a lively relationship
with God. It is hard to keep the faith when alone. We do better
in the company of other faithful folks.

To Ponder

To whom do you turn when you have important news, whether good or hard?

Where can you use support and counsel from other faithful people today?

Prayer

Advent Savior,
who comes to be with us,
we are heartened by the faithful friendship
of Mary and Elizabeth.
May they inspire us by their example
so that we too would accept the support of others
to help and encourage us in living by your priorities.
Amen.

Friday

And Mary said,
"My soul magnifies the Lord,
and my spirit rejoices in God my Savior,
for he has looked with favor on the lowliness of his servant.
Surely, from now on all generations will call me blessed;
For the Mighty One has done great things for me,
and holy is his name."
—Luke 1:46-49

Reflection

This is the beginning of Mary's Canticle of praise. It is worth comparing to Hannah's song (1 Samuel 2:1–1) and Zechariah's Canticle, which we already examined. She says this in response to the kind words of her relative Elizabeth, who has just spoken a blessing over Mary because of her obedience. This Canticle is often called the "Magnificat" and—like Zechariah's Canticle—is prayed every day by many Christians around the world, especially late in the day.

I love the juxtaposition in this excerpt. At one and the same time, Mary is able to identify both how God is intimately involved in her own life and how God is a performer of great deeds.

To Ponder

Where have you seen God work powerfully?

What do you need to be able to trust that God is at work in your life?

Prayer

Advent Savior,
who comes to be with us,
teach our souls to magnify you and rejoice in you.
Help us to see clearly where your power is already at work.
Amen.

Saturday

"He has shown strength with his arm;
he has scattered the proud in the thoughts of their hearts.
He has brought down the powerful from their thrones,
and lifted up the lowly;
he has filled the hungry with good things,
and sent the rich away empty."
—Luke 1:51–53

Reflection

These are daring and controversial words from a young teenage woman. They are a compelling vision of how God's work means huge and unexpected reversals: the proud and powerful and rich experience setbacks while the lowly and hungry receive blessings and fulfillment. No wonder some oppressive governments have at times forbidden Christians from reciting this canticle!

During Advent and Christmas, we sometimes settle for sentiment. Mary's song reminds us that God's coming has concrete implications—for our stomachs and our egos and our wallets. Advent is about the promises of God's justice.

To Ponder

Where do you see a need for God's justice and reversals?

Where does Mary's song convict you of the necessity for change and repentance?

Prayer

Advent Savior,
who comes to be with us,
it is easy to overlook concrete needs of so many people—
in our neighborhoods, communities, and around the world.
Give us a measure of your longing for compassion and justice
that we might not just pray Mary's song but live it out.
Amen.

Advent 4

John the Baptizer: The Voice in the Wilderness

… the word of God came to John …
—Luke 3:2

John the Baptizer is one of the more dramatic figures in the gospels, especially in our Advent texts. Not only is his birth miraculous, but he ends up living in the wilderness and wearing odd clothing and eating even stranger food. He is a prophet, in the line of Elijah we are told. We are not all called to reside in the wilderness as prophets. But all of us do need to hear God's words of challenge; Advent is not only about comfort.

Sunday

The child grew and became strong in spirit, and he was in the wilderness until the day he appeared publicly in Israel.
—Luke 1:80

Reflection

We do not know much about John's childhood, just as we do not know much about the childhood of Jesus. There are other parallels. Jesus, too, was a child who "grew and became strong" (Luke 1:40). And Jesus too was virtually anonymous until he "appeared publicly."

Even though John the Baptizer has a clear vocation from God, already predicted before his birth, he needs a long time of preparation and maturing. In John's case (like Moses and Elijah before him and Paul after him) this involves a lengthy stay in the wilderness, away from civilization.

To Ponder

How has God prepared you for your particular roles and responsibilities, your vocation?

Name a wilderness experience in your life.

Prayer

Advent Savior,
who comes to be with us,
you are passionately interested in each of us as your
children. Help us to rely on your Spirit to keep growing
into the people you long for us to be and the unique
vocation that you hope for each of us to embrace.
Amen.

Monday

*In the fifteenth year of the reign of Emperor Tiberius,
when Pontius Pilate was governor of Judea, and
Herod was ruler of Galilee and his brother Philip
ruler of the region of Ituraea and Trachonitis and
Lysanias ruler of Abilene, during the high priesthood
of Annas and Caiaphas, the word of God came to
John son of Zechariah in the wilderness.*
—Luke 3:1–2

Reflection

In this astonishing verse all the luminaries of the day are named,
along with their impressive titles—emperors of the earth, presidents
of superpowers, governors of vital regions, denominational heads
and cardinals and archbishops. These folks are not just in the
headlines, they make the news. But where does God's word come?
To lowly John, son of a little known priest Zechariah. And not in
a palace or castle or capitol but *in the wilderness*.

This text could not be clearer. While the world's attention is
on the great and famous, God's work and word often comes
through unimportant people. Just because you or I are not famous,
do not have much power, are not heeded by many, does not excuse
us from acting on God's behalf. In fact, such humble realities
might paradoxically increase our responsibility!

To Ponder

Name and describe an unexpected place or person where you heard from God.

Is there a situation right now that God might be calling you to address?

Prayer

Advent Savior,
who comes to be with us,
you keep showing up in surprising places and unlikely
ways. Help each of us discern where you are really at work
and truly speaking.
Amen.

Tuesday

He went into all the region around the Jordan,
proclaiming a baptism of repentance for the
forgiveness of sins, as it is written in the book of the
words of the prophet Isaiah,
"The voice of one crying out in the wilderness:
Prepare the way of the Lord,
make his paths straight. …
and all flesh shall see the salvation of God."
—Luke 3:3–4, 6

Reflection

John goes from being a quiet nobody in the boonies to a loud and challenging presence confronting people. He travels with his message and demands nothing less than repentance, turning around, conversion. This is all in the name of *preparing* for God's coming.

Zechariah, Elizabeth, Mary, and Joseph experience dramatic appearances from God's messengers. Even those righteous and dutiful folks are shaken, perplexed, and fearful. No wonder John warns the rest of us that we need special preparations to "see the salvation of God."

To Ponder

Are there particular habits or preoccupations that you need to set aside in order to be better prepared to obey God?

How have you responded in the past to prophetic types who challenged you to repent?

Prayer

Advent Savior,
who comes to be with us,
we want to prepare the way for your arrival and your
salvation but fear the cost, the price.
Give us the courage and conviction of John
that we might be willing to do what you require of us.
Amen.

Wednesday

*And the crowds asked him, "What then should we
do?" In reply he said to them, "anyone who has two
coats must share with one who has none; and
whoever has food must do likewise."*
—Luke 3:10–11

Reflection

While John makes religious demands on people—repent, be
baptized—the crowds realize this is not enough. When they press
him for counsel, he speaks about undertaking a compassionate
lifestyle. We are to share from the abundance of our possessions
and food with those in need.

Given the affluence of our culture and—let's face it—my own
abundance, I find John's words particularly challenging. God does
not let me rest easy in my comfort.

To Ponder

Who are the needy that God is challenging you to show compassion and justice?

Where are you finding it particularly hard to obey God's call?

Prayer

Advent Savior,
who comes to be with us,
how shall we live to prepare for your coming
and to honor your priorities?
Help us to take seriously your challenges
so that we might live lives
that demonstrate your justice and compassion.
Amen.

Thursday

Even tax collectors came to be baptized, and they asked him, "Teacher, what should we do?" He said to them, "Collect no more than the amount prescribed for you." Soldiers also asked him, "And we, what should we do?" He said to them, "Do not extort money from anyone by threats or false accusation, and be satisfied with your wages."
—Luke 3:12–14

Reflection

This is a curious passage. Tax collectors and soldiers (employees of Rome, the occupying empire) were particularly loathed. Their occupations were often corrupt. Yet John does not counsel them to abandon their jobs. Rather, he advises them to act with honor, to be law abiding, to be contented. He challenges them to be different than their co-workers.

Each of us must examine the question that tax collectors and soldiers asked: "What should we do?" Chances are that there are demanding faith implications for us—whether in our home, at school, in our jobs, as part of our volunteer commitments.

To Ponder

Name some temptations in your life today.

Where might you live and act differently than your peers, not for the sake of being different but to honor God's priorities?

Prayer

Advent Savior,
who comes to be with us,
we are more like oppressive tax collectors and corrupt
soldiers than we would like to admit.
Yet for us too you offer grace and new ways to live.
Amen.

Friday

*As the people were filled with expectation, and all
were questioning in their hearts concerning John,
whether he might be the Messiah, John answered all
of them by saying, "I baptize you with water; but
one who is more powerful than I is coming; I am not
worthy to untie the thong of his sandals. He will
baptize you with the Holy Spirit and fire."*
—Luke 3:15–16

Reflection

John speaks with passion, authority, and conviction. But he always understands that the message is not about him. His priority is to point elsewhere, to prepare people for encountering Jesus.

Wherever we are located, whatever our job or vocation, whichever role we inhabit, ultimately the most important challenge before us is to help orient people around us to God and God's Reign. Nothing else finally matters.

To Ponder

How can your sphere of involvements be a place where people are oriented towards God?

What distracts you from putting God first?

Prayer

Advent Savior,
who comes to be with us,
John spoke up courageously for your priorities.
Help us to know how to speak on your behalf wherever we are. Amen.

Saturday

So with many other exhortations, he proclaimed the good news to the people. But Herod the ruler who had been rebuked by him because of Herodias, his brother's wife and because of all the evil things Herod had done, added to them all by shutting up John in prison.
—Luke 3:18–20

Reflection

There are perplexing paradoxes in this passage. First, John's harsh words about repentance and a "winnowing fork" and burning chaff "with unquenchable fire" (Luke 3:17) are called "good news!" Sounds sobering to me. Second, all John's faithful work ends up with him being imprisoned and, ultimately, killed. The third paradox is implied. Somehow John has to leave the scene before Jesus can appear and do his ministry.

In God's upside down kingdom, many expectations are turned on their head. The way for good news can sometimes be cleared only by first hearing realistic bad news. Our faithful actions do not always result in prosperity or success; they may end in persecution and misunderstanding. And the most important things that we can do often mean putting others first.

To Ponder

Where have you paid an unexpectedly high price for faithfulness?

Where are you tempted to tone down and sugar coat the good news?

Prayer

Advent Savior,
who comes to be with us,
John sets a challenging example of serving your priorities,
even at great cost to himself.
May our prayers this Advent contribute to and reinforce
our commitment to your coming reign.
Amen.

Notes

Notes

Start the New Year with the Church Health Center's new daily devotional *Have a Blessed Day*! Find *Have a Blessed Day* on **www.ChurchHealthCenter.org/Store** to give this gift at Christmas.